the OPEN DOOR

PAINTINGS AND POETRY

BY XNADU

The Heart of Reality blooms
In gardens most fair —
Through worlds in chaos comes a newness —
Born in the debris of illusion and disillusion
Comes the Glorious Dawn —
Arriving to meet the conflict of changing ages —
Making new balances keyed to birth —
New tones of melodies unknown to Earth dimension —
Placing pathways unvisioned to the consciousness of man —
A New Door opens —

She rises in mist from the shadowy deeps
Cloaking in Her splendor myriad treasures of past Eons
Too ancient for numbering —
She calls in song all measure of men and things
Heralding once more Her arrival for renewal of all life.

Her long tresses She dips in the foam of Infinity's Cauldron
And hangs it to dry
Making a pathway of Light for the Wee Ones —
Her expressions of love
That prepare all worlds for new life —
Dipping into the sea
She raises the currents of joy and sets them on a new path —
Again and again She dips
Each time reactivating the many streams
And channeling each in a new direction
For the beginning flow for Her New Golden Age
Of Perfection — Reality — and Truth —
The misdirected are redeemed
And take their place in the new design for the new creation —
Old forms are swallowed up in the new —
The past becomes the beginning present
Set in lacy patterns that permit never before treasures
To be found and formed.

For manifested Reality begins its play of action
Her children — the enactors — take their places
At each long golden tube that leads each stream from there to here
She makes ready for the journey in building their new bodies
forms and gifts — as embodied enactments
For placing Her New Golden Age —

Yes — Let me warm myself in the sunset of your smile —
My Beloved One —
Hold me dearly lest I fade away before my time of coming forth!
I bask always in your glory, Beautious One —
Hope breeds eternally in my heart a poem of Presences so Real —
Yet so elusive to the touch —
A child chosen for a destiny too vast for knowing —
Yet somehow played and placed in the vacuum called Time —
Let me not dream or sleep for I feel upon me the value
of using each moment in awareness —
I feel most acutely my limitations but know in spite of these —
that beyond me — "Will Be Done" —
Let me not indulge what I seek most — the moments of Wholeness
given in this space of time of my usefulness —
Help me to free even this holding —
That I may be more useful to the needs of my calling —
Truly my chaffing is a Blessing —

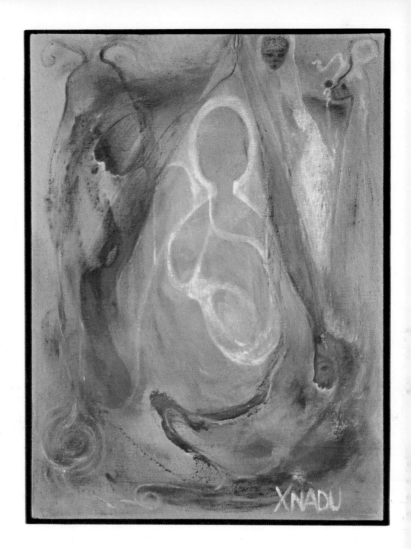

Born in the cave of the Heart
Nurtured on Love —
I came forth on the Light of Truth
I am The Eternal One

Glorious High Plateau of Divine Vision —
Manifesting the Perfection
Rainbow Hues enfold The Path —
The Mount of Glory in sight —

The Starry Vault gives back its own —
The Wholeness made — They shall abide —
The Twinship Throne from on High —
Descends near Earth this season tide
To celebrate The Glory Old —
Forever retold in the fresh new ways —
Ever young —
Bringing Hope and Light for All —
Behold!
The Miracle of Birth!

Reality Land
This realm —
Crossing the Great Abyss
The dark Truth in velvet feeling penetrates —

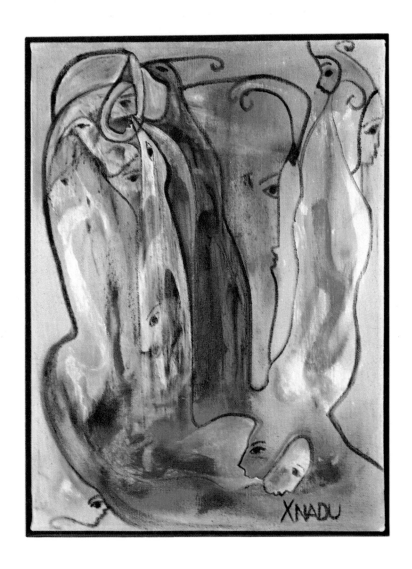

Glorious Master Spirit —
Tamer of all force flows in all worlds
Brings the blending in a new Unity —
The stream of life released again —

Angelic songs She sings —
Angelic forms to bring anew —
Bringing life's music —
Long forgotten
In locked realms of Light —
Unfurled rainbow paths
With cherubs dancing gleely on winged clouds —
Dew drops kissing Her hair of flame —
Bringing harmonies ages old
In sounds most glorious —
T-Ruth Her name
Love — Her game —

The Christmas Spirit comes once a year —
To renew the flow of Love and good cheer —
A herald of tidings old — But ever new —
A gift from lighted worlds of Love for All.

By the stream of Eternity's own garden —
Lies a secret hidden —
Yet known —
'Tis a dream of Reality written in life's key —
Unavailable until truly sought —
By One who wishes to know —
So near — you can touch it with Vision —
But the merging is that to be —
Learn to allow —
Humility is an important key —

Divine Lady — Mirrors The Child of Spaceless Vision —
The Spirit of Truth exalts the Path —
Making new lines of clarity —
Coming forth —

Unmasking the new forms —
The King of Love trods the many realms —
Bringing a newness to all worlds —
Light comes
Anew —

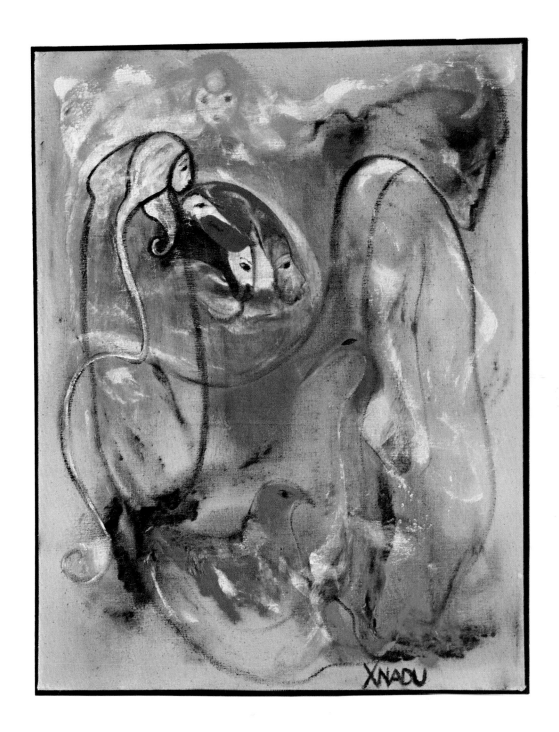

In the silence of Reality —
Dwells a new land — long hidden —
Undiscovered yet known in the True Space —
Coming forth thru chaotic upheaval and confusion —
Bringing a visioned wholeness —

The Lady of Wisdom comes forth in gentle splendor —
Heralding a new era of Wholeness and Balance
Through the green gold of Earth —
She brings mysteries available and longing for fulfillment —
Greet Her —
Welcome Her —

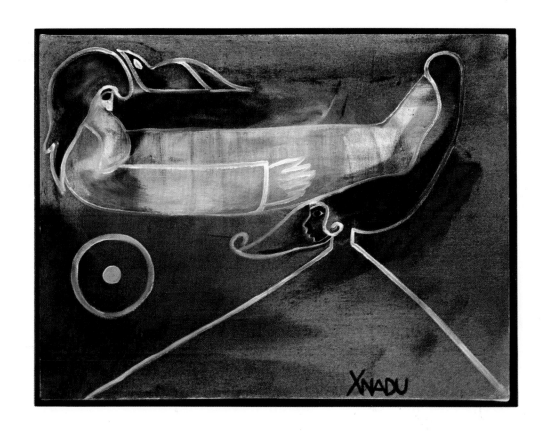

The Christ Flow Overhead
Brings recognitions of coming events —
A preparatory help for future actions —

The Lady of Truth brings the Door of Glory —
Open wide — in a blaze of Golden Light —
Bringing the Pyramid of Wholeness —
Calling All —
Come Forth —
Bear the Reality of True Knowing —

The
Trinity of Hope
Emerges in clarity of Vision —
The
Miracle of Peace —
Performs its image upon Earth —

The Firey Vault of Love descends from On High
Bringing Cosmic Purification
A Firey bath for new formulas on Earth —
The Flame of Love
Embodied Anew —

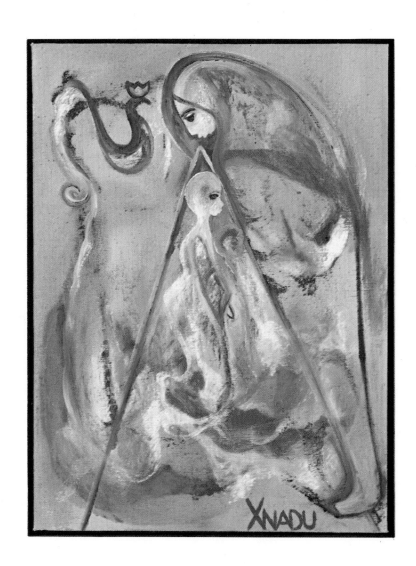

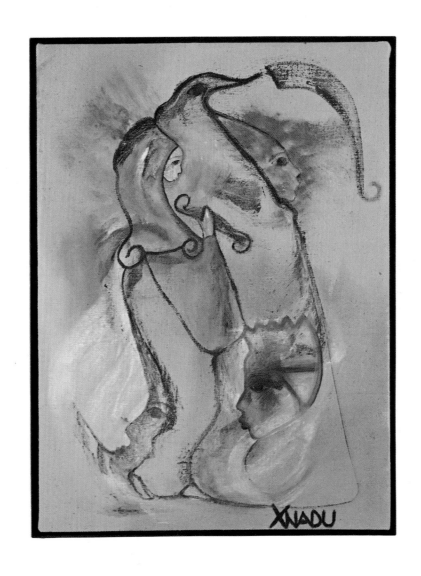

Lovely Lady of the Rainbow Land
Brings the scroll of revealed Truths
Now opened for Earth flows

A golden Center of flow
Blazes forth to balance past forms —
Lending design for Clarity

Bringing Her court of Reality
Unmasking Truth
She of Vision
Unlocks the masked ball

26

Virgin Lady —
Naked Truth —
Clothed in the splendor of Golden Light —
Sheds Her gifts of radiant glory
To all —

And ore the hills came a running
A small Wee One of clarey hue
    No taller than my thumb
A shouting a poem of meter true
    A hearald of the new
A twinkle dawn — a comin'
The mist is agathering for the True —

Winged Love —
A Child of golden hue —
Bringing a gentle blue fused flow —
Creativity catalysts anew —

Mystic Worlds Unfold —
The Light Unveils
The Green Door offers a way
   To these vistas of Celestial Beauty —

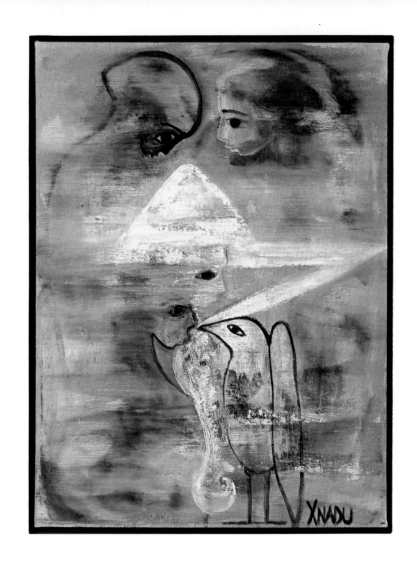

The Pyramid of Light unfolds in balance —
The Wholeness of Revelation —
Bringing New Cosmic Force Flows
Prepare to Embody Them!

Additional copies of this book may be obtained by writing
The Open Door, Box 3703, Carmel, California 93921